JULIETTE LOW
Founder of the Girl Scouts of America

By June Behrens

CHILDRENS PRESS ®

CHICAGO

Girl Scouts pull a supply cart on a camping trip in the 1920s.

DEDICATION
To my granddaughter
Lyndee Johnson

Library of Congress Cataloging-in-Publication Data

Behrens, June.
    Juliette Gordon Low: Founder of the Girl Scouts of
America / by June Behrens.
        p.   cm. — (Picture story biography)
    Summary: Depicts the life of the vigorous and
unconventional woman from Savannah who founded the
American branch of the Girl Scouts.
    ISBN 0-516-04171-1
    1.   Low, Juliette Gordon, 1860-1927—Juvenile
literature.   2.   Girl Scouts—United States—Biography—
Juvenile literature.   3.   Girl Scouts of the United States of
America—Biography—Juvenile literature.   [1. Low,
Juliette Gordon, 1860-1927. 2. Girl Scouts. of the
United States of America—Biography.]   I. Title.
II. Series.
HS3359.L6B45   1988
369.46'3'0924—dc19   88-11976
[B]   CIP
[92]   AC

Childrens Press®, Chicago
Copyright ©1988 by Regensteiner Publishing Enterprises, Inc.
All rights reserved. Published simultaneously in Canada.
Printed in the United States of America.
    5 6 7 8 9 10 R 97 96 95 94

Daisy (Juliette) Low as she looked in 1914, two years after she started the Girl Guides.

"I've got something for the girls of Savannah and all America and all the world and we're going to start it tonight!" Daisy Low announced. She had just come back to town. No one knew that her latest wild idea—organizing the Girl Guides—would become the Girl Scouts of America.

The people of Savannah wondered about the Girl Guides. Still they thought it might be all right if their daughters joined the group. After all, "Though Daisy might be odd in some ways, she was a Gordon, and undeniably a lady."

So on March 12, 1912, eighteen girls signed up for Daisy's program. Daisy set up the first Girl Guide headquarters in her carriage house.

Daisy was born into the Gordon family in 1860. She grew up during the Civil War. It was a world of soldiers and fighting men. Her father was Confederate Captain William Gordon, a southerner. Her mother was Eleanor Kinzie Gordon, a northerner.

The Gordons lived in Savannah, Georgia. They had a lively household of four daughters and two sons.

Six-year-old Daisy (right) lived with her brothers and sisters in the Gordon family home.

Alice (left),
Daisy (center),
and Willie (right)
Gordon

Daisy was christened Juliette. But she did not keep her name for long. "I'll bet this one will be a daisy," said an observant uncle. From then on, Juliette was known as Daisy.

Daisy had a happy childhood after the Civil War. Life was filled with the fun and activities of a large family. The children enjoyed games and play acting. On summer vacations the family went boating and fishing. Daisy rode horses and played tennis well. She liked to draw pictures and write poetry, too.

Mable (left),
Eleanor (center),
and Daisy (right)
Gordon

Daisy had a wild imagination. She was daring and would try anything. Her sister Eleanor called her "Crazy Daisy." She did and said the unexpected, entertaining everyone. Her mother said these antics were "Daisy's stunts."

Daisy was an excellent swimmer. When she was eight, she rescued a little boy who had fallen into the water. Daisy didn't talk about her brave deed. But her mother found out when she asked Daisy about her wet clothes.

All her life Daisy loved and cared for animals. She brought home stray cats and dogs. She nursed injured birds back to health. She wanted to help any person or animal in distress. Daisy had an overflowing kindness about her. Her favorite pets were her dogs, her mockingbirds, and her beloved parrot, Polly Poons.

At nine Daisy was small and thin. She had light brown hair and brown eyes. She worried about her freckled "pointy" nose. She once said, "My Mama says I am as ugly as ten bears!"

Daisy attended West Hull Street School in Savannah

At thirteen Daisy went away to boarding school in Virginia. She liked drawing and reading good books. She was the first to tell how awful she was in spelling and math.

After boarding school Daisy went to Charbonnier's School, a finishing school for young ladies in New York City. There, Daisy continued to work on her drawing and painting. At school all classes were taught in French. Daisy's younger brother George Arthur once told her not to write letters home in French any more, "because you can't spell in French, either!"

Daisy, her classmates, and teachers at Edge Hill Academy in Charlottesville, Virginia

A grown-up and very fashionable Daisy poses for the camera.

After finishing at Charbonnier's School, Daisy returned home. At her coming-out party she blossomed into a true Savannah belle. Her sparkle and quick wit charmed her friends. Daisy was pretty and loved parties and people. She had many young admirers.

The Gordons sent Daisy on a trip to Europe. They asked her to call on a family friend, Andrew Low. Low was a wealthy Englishman. He also had a home in Savannah. Daisy visited the Low family. She became good friends with Andrew Low's son and daughters.

On her return to Savannah Daisy's life was carefree. She traveled and visited relatives and friends. She went to parties and renewed old friendships.

Two years after her first visit, Daisy returned to England. She stayed with the Lows. Her friendship with Andrew's son, William, grew. Daisy and Willie fell in love. William—Daisy called him Billow—was handsome. His friends were important and wealthy members of British high society.

William Low came to America to meet Daisy's family. The Gordon family announced Daisy's engagement to William Low. They planned a grand wedding. It was the social event of the season. On

Daisy and William Low with their wedding party

December 21, 1886 Daisy (Juliette) Gordon of Savannah, Georgia became the bride of William Low of Warwickshire, England.

The excitement of the day turned to tragedy. As Daisy and Billow ran through a hail of rice thrown by wedding guests, a grain of rice lodged in Daisy's ear. An infection resulted, causing Daisy to become deaf in that ear. She already had suffered severe hearing loss in her other ear the year before.

For the rest of her life Daisy was deaf. Her behavior was sometimes strange. She didn't always understand what people said. Daisy explained that she was such a ''talker'' because ''it is just too much work trying so hard to listen all the time.''

After the wedding Daisy and Billow lived in Savannah. But after a few months Billow wanted to go home to England. Now Daisy became an English woman as well as an American. She lived in both countries all her life.

In England Daisy became the belle of English society. She entertained British lords and ladies. Daisy introduced Southern hospitality and cooking to her new friends. Visitors came to see Billow and Daisy in their homes in England and Scotland.

Many of their friends were famous. Billow and Daisy knew the Prince of Wales. He later became King Edward VII of Great Britain. Daisy argued with young Winston Churchill at a dinner party. She went fishing with Rudyard Kipling. Daisy was presented to Queen Victoria.

Rudyard Kipling became one of Daisy's closest friends. They shared a love for animals and children. When they were together, they kept the guests at parties laughing.

Rudyard Kipling (left). As was the custom in British society, Daisy was presented to Queen Victoria at court.

Daisy's life was filled with parties and travel. Back and forth she went to her homes in the United States, England, and Scotland.

When the Spanish-American war broke out, Daisy left Billow and hurried home to Savannah. Daisy was there to help. General Gordon served in the military, with sons Bill and Arthur as his aides. Daisy and her mother cared for the sick. The family was commended by the President of the United States.

William and Eleanor Kinzie Gordon, Daisy's parents

Daisy sculpted the head (left) of her niece, Daisy Gordon Lawrence (right).

However, things were not going well with Billow and Daisy. They began to do fewer and fewer things together. Billow traveled with his friends. Daisy took her own trips. She went to Egypt with her sister Mabel. She made friends wherever she went.

Daisy returned to her art work. She painted and sculpted. She wrote poetry. Daisy learned how to be a blacksmith. She made the wrought iron gates for her home. Daisy had no children, but she kept busy.

Daisy and Billow grew farther apart. They decided to divorce.

Billow became very ill and died before the divorce became final. Daisy felt more alone than ever. She returned to her home in Savannah.

Daisy felt her life was empty. She needed something to live for. She wrote to her mother, "I am just an idle woman of the world, with no real work or duties. I would like to get away from the world somewhere and work at sculpturing . . . start to do some work in life."

Daisy filled her life with more travel and new adventures. She visited India. She wanted to see the places her friend Kipling had written about. She was one of the first women to fly in a monoplane. Her brother once said, "She would try

Daisy and Rudyard Kipling loved adventure, and flying was a grand new adventure.

anything, particularly if she had never attempted it before.''

Daisy went to Paris to learn more about sculpture. At the time she never realized that her interest in art would change her life.

When she returned to England, Daisy met General Sir Robert Baden-Powell. He was a hero of the Boer War. He was a sculptor, also. Daisy and Baden-Powell shared their art work and interests. Daisy

Lord and Lady Baden-Powell helped Daisy (right) bring scouting to America.

wrote home, "He (Baden-Powell) is a genius as a soldier and he draws, paints and models as well. He left the army . . . to organize the Boy Scouts and now he has forty thousand boys all over Great Britain, with branches in the U.S.A., France, and Germany."

Baden-Powell told Daisy about the Girl Guides. Like the Boy Scouts, the girls took part in worthwhile activities. They learned new things and helped others.

18

Baden-Powell's sister, Agnes Baden-Powell, was their leader.

Daisy wanted to help. She wrote to her family, "I like girls and I like the organization and the rules and pastimes, so if you find that I get very deeply interested, you must not be surprised."

At her home in Scotland Daisy organized a group of seven girls. She taught her Girl Guides home skills and hiking. They learned ways to make money at home. Daisy always had a tea party with special cakes for her girls.

Scout leader teaches a young girl how to operate foot treadle sewing machine. Daisy "loved" the uniforms she designed for her guides.

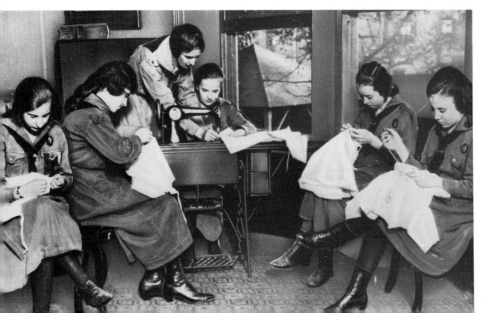

Daisy stands with one of her first Girl Guides patrols.

Daisy returned to London. She started two more troops of Girl Guides. What a grand new adventure. Daisy had at last found worthwhile work for herself.

Daisy came to America with a plan for the girls in Savannah. She traveled on the same ship with Baden-Powell. He was on a world tour to promote the Boy Scout movement. He helped Daisy with her plan for Girl Guides in America.

Daisy wasted no time getting things started. The carriage house behind Daisy's home became headquarters. Two patrols of Girl Guides were begun. Daisy and her leaders planned the uniforms. They organized activities and projects.

News of the Girl Guides spread. People from other states asked about the program. Daisy had a dream. She wanted to see Girl Guides in every state. Daisy was happier than she had ever been. She had searched the world over for a purpose in life. Daisy had found it.

Daisy went to work getting her Girl Guides organized nationally. She called on her important friends. She told them about the Girl Guide movement. The wives of two United States presidents helped. Society leaders came through for Daisy's

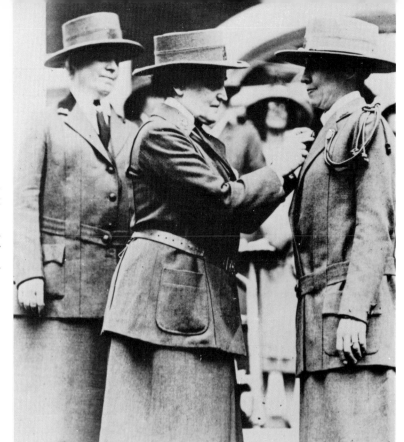

Daisy pins a tenderfoot badge on Mrs. Coolidge. Mrs. Hoover stands at left.

girls. Soon hundreds of women were helping Daisy's program.

Daisy started calling her Guides the Girl Scouts. She published a handbook. She set up headquarters in Washington, D.C. Girl Scouting spread across America. Daisy became the first president.

Daisy's first National Board of Councilors for Girl Scouts included many important women.

Daisy Low became known all over the United States. She was a celebrity!

Back in England Daisy was presented to Queen Mary. She saw her old friend Baden-Powell. He couldn't believe Girl Scouting had grown so fast in America. He knew Daisy and her many friends had made this possible. No one said "no" when Daisy asked for help. If they did, she didn't hear them.

Theodore Roosevelt started the National Park system in America. He actively supported the scouting program.

England had entered World War I. Daisy helped with British war relief. She carried on with her Girl Scout work. Back in America, Daisy's mother wrote to the family, "Daisy's Scouts are booming! She has now 7,000 registered, and she's doing many wonderful stunts for them." Daisy moved the National Girl Scout

In 1916 Daisy moved The Girl Scout National Headquarters to New York (left). At election time, Girl Scouts watched babies so mothers could vote.

Headquarters from Washington to New York. A friend told Daisy she should stop paying all the bills. From the beginning Daisy had paid the rent and salaries. She had bought handbooks and uniforms. She paid her own expenses when traveling to tell people about Girl Scouting. Daisy had even sold her pearls to pay the bills for her beloved Girl Scouts!

The United States entered World War I in 1917. Girl Scouts served in many ways. They helped with nursing. They sold Liberty Bonds and tended victory gardens. Juliette Low traveled across the country giving speeches. She brought young and old into the movement.

In 1919 members of the Girl Guides of England and the Girl Scouts of America met in London. They called attention to world peace. Juliette Low was there to represent

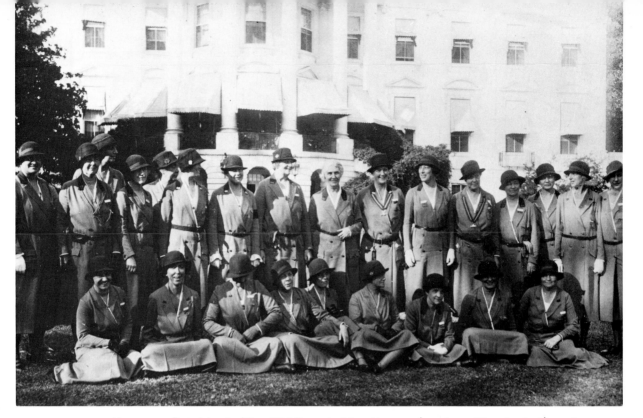

Honorary President of the Girl Scouts Mrs. Hoover (center without a hat), met with the National Executive committee at the White House.

the Girl Scouts in America. She proudly reported there were 40,000 girls in the program.

Juliette Low stepped down as president in 1920. Her new title was "The Founder." Her birthday, October 31, became Girl Scout Founder's Day. Daisy took on a new job, to organize a worldwide Girl Scout movement.

Mrs. Herbert Hoover became

Daisy was at the first World Camp. She never let her deafness keep her from communicating with people of all ages.

president of Girl Scouts in 1922. That year a World Camp was started in London. Daisy wanted girls from around the world to come to the United States.

In 1926 Daisy's dream came true. Sir Baden-Powell and his wife joined Daisy in the United States. They welcomed girls to the World Camp. Girl Scouts from many countries came. They pledged themselves to world peace.

Juliette Low died on January 17, 1927 in Savannah. She had been very ill for a long time. But Daisy had lived to see her beloved Girl Scout movement become a worldwide organization with thousands and thousands of members.

In 1974, Jimmy Carter, governor of Georgia, unveiled the Juliette Low sculpture in the Georgia State Capitol Hall of Fame.

Girl Scouts still learn
camping (above), cooking,
and sailing skills.

WORDS ABOUT JULIETTE LOW*

Brother Arthur Gordon: *"She (Daisy) had a vision . . . of what Girl Scouting would mean for our American Girls . . . She gave to the Girl Scouts every particle of her will power and intelligence and interest and vitality."*

Brother Arthur Gordon: *"She was not only very entertaining and amusing when she desired to be, but she was frequently killingly funny, when she had no intention of being fully funny at all!"*

Rose Kerr: *"She was unique. There is not, there never can have been anyone exactly like her. And as for guessing what she would think or say about anything, you might just as well have tried to forecast the path of a whirlwind."*

Rose Kerr: *"Imagine a woman, delicate, no longer young, with no great fortune, handicapped by deafness, deliberately setting out to conquer the United States for Girl Guiding!"*

Rose Kerr: *"She was the rarest of human beings, an original thinker; she had a fresh and unbiased approach to any problem."*

Nephew Rowland Leigh: *"Her methods were as curious and attractive as those of Alice in Wonderland, the results equally astounding but far more useful. She tackled the impossible with carefree vitality, overcoming the toughest obstacles by blandly ignoring them."*

Eleanor Nash McWilliam: *"She did not live alone in her world of silence. She brought the outer world into it with the force of her personality and wit. To her, life itself was really the Great Adventure."*

Eleanor Nash McWilliam: *"She was the person I most liked to be with."*

Josephine Daskam Bacon (on Daisy Low and her uniform): *"She loved that big hat; she loved that ridiculous whistle; she loved her whole uniform! . . . she was an eternal girl. And so she could drench with her vitality and enthusiasm the little plant she had brought over from England, and cherish it 'til it grew into the great tree it is today."*

Anne Hyde Choate: *"During the last years of her life, her heart sang with the feeling that this movement was bringing joy and happiness to many girls in the land and a feeling of sisterhood toward the girls of all nations . . . "*

Josephine Bacon: *"If succeeding leaders light their fires from the glowing fire of Juliette Low's enthusiasm, those fires will never die!"*

* Quotes from *Juliette Low and the Girl Scouts,* Choate and Ferris
Published by Girl Scouts, New York, 1928

JULIETTE LOW

TIMELINE

1860	October 31—born in Savannah, Georgia; second of six children of William Gordon and Eleanor (Kinzie) Gordon
1867-68	Attended West Hull Street School, Savannah
1877	Graduated from Edge Hill Academy, Charlottesville, Virginia
1877	Attended Charbonnier's School, New York City
1882	Took first trip to Europe and met William Low
1886	Married William Low in Savannah
1887	Moved with her husband to Wellesbourne House, Warwickshire, England
1898	Joined the Gordon family in Florida to help the Spanish-American War relief
1905	Widowed by the death of her husband, William Low
1911	Met Sir Robert Baden-Powell and learned of the Girl Guides movement
1912	March 12—Organized first Girl Guides in Savannah
1913	Opened National Headquarters in Washington, D.C. and changed name of organization from Girl Guides to Girl Scouts of America
1916	Moved National Headquarters to New York City
1912-20	Traveled throughout the United States promoting Girl Scouting in America
1917	United States entered into World War I; Mrs. Woodrow Wilson named the first honorary president of Girl Scouts
1920	Retired as president and honored with title of Founder, Girl Scouts of U.S.A. Her birthday, October 31 declared Girl Scout Founder's Day
1920	Organized first International Conference of Girl Guides and Girl Scouts held in Oxford, England
1926	Organized first International Conference of Girl Guides and Girl Scouts held in the U.S.A.; Twenty-nine countries are represented
1927	January 17—Juliette Low died in Savannah
1944	Liberty ship S.S. Juliette Low launched in Savannah
1948	U.S. postage stamp for Juliette Gordon Low printed
1973	Juliette Low portrait presented to the National Gallery in Washington, D.C.
1974	Juliette Low bust placed in Georgia State Capitol Hall of Fame
1983	Office building named Juliette Gordon Low Federal Complex opened in Savannah, Georgia

The Girl Scout movement has touched the lives of almost 52 million women. Many of the women leaders today were at one time Girl Scouts. Girl Scouting is the world's largest voluntary organization. Daisy (Juliette) Low started it all.

ABOUT THE AUTHOR

For the past 25 years June Behrens has been writing for children. Her many years as an educator have made her sensitive to the interests and needs of young readers. Mrs. Behrens has written over 60 books, touching on a wide range of subjects in both fiction and nonfiction. June Behrens received her academic education from the University of California at Santa Barbara, where she was honored as Distinguished Alumni of the Year for her contributions to the field of education. She has a Master's degree from the University of Southern California. Mrs. Behrens is listed in *Who's Who of American Women*. She lives with her husband in Rancho Palos Verdes, near Los Angeles.